XI'AN

西安

FOREIGN LANGUAGES PRESS   BEIJING

外文出版社　北京

Xi'an

    As one of the four great nations with an ancient civilization in the world, China established many famous historical and cultural towns during its long history. Xi'an was one of the six ancient capitals in China and was the greatest among them.

    Xi'an is located in Shaanxi Province, lying in the middle of the Guanzhong Plain with the Qinling Mountains to the north and the Weihe River to the south. Here, the rivers are winding and the climate is good, so that it is known as the "Continental Sea" and "Natural Grain Store". Since ancient times, it has been a piece of rich land suitable for human habitation. In the long prehistoric period, the Xi'an area played an important role as the origin of Chinese civilization because of its location in the center of the Yellow River Civilization Area. According to archaeological finds, "Lantian Man", who was already able to obtain simple living materials, appeared in Xi'an area as early as 800,000 years ago; in 6000 B. C., there came into being primitive matriarchal villages with "Banpo Village" as their representative.

"It has been the land of emperors since ancient times." Due to its perfect natural geographical conditions and the rapid development of civilization, the Xi'an area became the center of the country's political power in the early years. It was called Chang'an in ancient times, and was the capital of 11 dynasties, including the Western Zhou Dynasty (c. 11th century-771 B. C.), Qin Dynasty (221-206 B. C.), Western Han Dynasty (206 B. C.-A. D. 25), Sui Dynasty (518-618), and Tang Dynasty (618-907). Xi'an was a city which had the longest history as a capital for 1,000 years. In the history of world cities, the architectural scale of Chang'an in the Han Dynasty was three times bigger than that of ancient Roman; Chang'an in the Tang Dynasty was the largest and busiest international metropolis in the world as well as the terminal of the "Silk Road" which connected Europe and Asia for trade and cultural exchanges. In this brilliant period of history, the Xi'an area formed a great cultural heritage, and the ancient capital Xi'an had witnessed the historical changes of Chinese civilization from the beginning to its prosperity.

Today, Xi'an is the capital of Shaanxi Province as well as the biggest city in Northwest China. The Xi'an area was regarded as the "Chinese Museum of Nature and History" because of its long history, rich culture and beautiful scenery. On this piece of land are many buildings of different dynasties, such as the ruins of Efang Palace of the Qin Dynasty, Weiyang Palace of the Han Dynasty and Daming Palace of the Tang Dynasty; worshippers frequently visit sites like Xingjiao Temple, Qinglong Temple, Xingshan Temple and the Great Mosque; the Greater and Lesser Wild Goose Pagodas of the Tang Dynasty, the Bell and Drum Towers and the City Walls of the Ming Dynasty still stand there; there are always many visitors to the Steles Forest, Xingqing Palace Park, Huaqing Pond and Mount Lishan. Here are concentrated many imperial tombs, like the Qin, Han and Tang Tombs. Of them, the tomb of Qinshihuang (the First Emperor of the Qin), in which the terra-cotta army was discovered and is on display, is the most attractive and has been cited as the "Eighth Wonder in the World".

Xi'an is a place of culture and one of the best tourist cities in China. After experiencing thousands of years of changes, it still fascinates the eyes of tourists. Walking in the streets of the old city, you may easily be attracted by historical remains, traditional culture and unique lifestyles, enough for you to taste their endless flavors.

西　安

　　世界四大文明古国之一的中国,以其悠久的历史孕育出众多的历史文化名城,中国六大古都之一的西安,更是名城中的翘楚。

　　西安位于中国陕西省境内,地处关中平原中部,南依秦岭,北临渭河,四周曲水环绕,气候适宜,素有"陆海"、"天府"之誉。自远古时期起,这里就是一片适于人类栖居的天然沃土。在漫长的史前时期,西安地区因地处中华黄河流域文明的中心区域而扮演了文明发祥地的重要角色。据考古挖掘证实,早在80万年前,西安地区已出现了能够获取简单生活资料的"蓝田猿人";在公元前6000年左右产生了以"半坡遗址"为代表的母系氏族原始村落。

　　"秦中自古帝王州"。优越的自然地理条件加上文明的迅速繁衍,使西安地区很早就成为国家政权统治中心。西安古称长安,自西周(约前11世纪—前771年)起,先后有秦(前221—前206年)、西汉(前206—公元25年)、隋(581—618年)、唐(618—907年)等十一个王朝在此建都,历时千年,是中国历史上建都时间最长的一座城市。在世界城市史上,汉都长安的建筑规模曾是古罗马城的三倍;唐都长安是当时世界上最大、最繁华的国际大都会,同时是沟通欧亚经济文化的"丝绸之路"的起点。在这段辉煌的历史时期中,西安地区缔造了丰厚的文化遗产,古都西安也成为华夏文明从萌芽成长到强盛的历史缩影。

如今的西安市是陕西省省会，也是中国西北地区最大的城市。西安地区因其悠久的历史、丰富的人文景观被人们誉为"中国天然历史博物馆"。在这片古老的土地上，历代建筑遗迹遍布，秦阿房宫、汉未央宫、唐大明宫等宫阙遗址引人发幽古之思；兴教寺、青龙寺、兴善寺、大清真寺等寺庙内香火依然；唐代的大雁塔、小雁塔，明代的钟楼、鼓楼、城墙巍峨耸立；碑林、兴庆宫公园、华清池、骊山游人如织。历代皇家陵墓中的秦陵、汉陵、唐陵在此地最为集中，其中秦始皇陵兵马俑的发现和展出，轰动了世界，被称为"世界第八大奇迹"。

　　西安是一个极富文化旅游传统的地方，在历尽千年沧桑后，至今仍积聚着神奇的魅力。当人们漫步古都街头的时候，常常会被这些历史遗迹、传统文化和独具特色的生活方式所吸引，品味其绵绵的余韵。

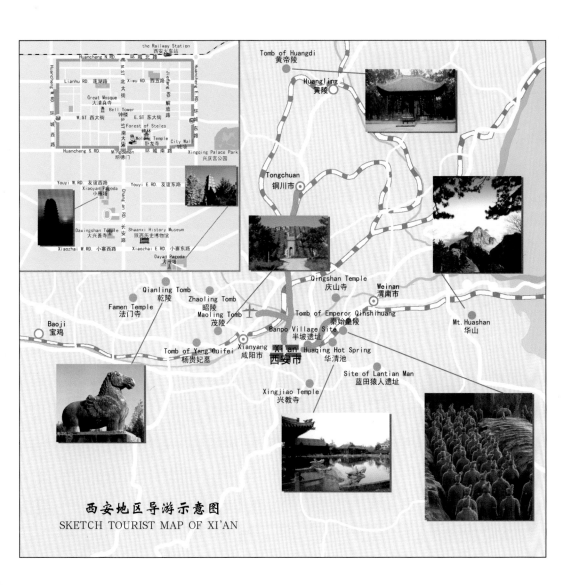

Xi'an

Known as Fengjing, Gaojing and
Chang'an in ancient times, Xi'an
got its present name in the 14th
century. Today's Xi'an City has ju-
risdiction over 7 districts and 6
counties in an area of 9,900 square
kilometers and with a population of
6 million.

西安

西安古称丰京、镐京、长安等,14 世纪
才定名为西安。如今的西安市下辖 7
区 6 县,面积 9900 余平方公里,人口
600 余万。

City Wall

The city wall of Xi'an is one of the ancient city walls well-preserved in China. The extant city wall of Xi'an was first built in early Ming Dynasty (1368-1644) and was renovated in recent years. The city wall is 12 to 15 meters high and 12 to 14 meters wide at the top. Its circumsference is 14.6 kilometers, enclosing an area of 3.5 square kilometers. Outside the city wall is a moat, which has now been opened as a round-the-city park.

城垣

西安城垣是中国现存规模最大、保存最完好的古城墙建筑之一。现存西安城垣始建于明(1368－1644年)初,近年来整修一新。城墙高12米至15米,顶宽12米至14米,周长14.6公里,面积3.5平方公里。城墙外环有一条护城河,现已辟为环城公园。

City Gate

There are east, west, south and north gate towers on the four sides of the city wall. The city gate tower is formed by a main tower, an arrow tower and an enceinte, showing the way of fending off enemy besieging in ancient wars.

城门

西安城墙四面设有东、西、南、北四座高大雄伟的城门。城门由正楼、箭楼和瓮城组成，显示出它在古代战时的御敌功用。

City Scene ▷

The city layout of ancient times can still be seen in today's Xi'an City. The city is criss-crossed by straight main streets like a chess-board. This picture shows South Street in the center of the city.

西安市景

今日的西安城仍依稀可辨昔日王都的城市格局，城中主干道皆为横平竖直的通衢大道。图为位于市中心区的南大街。

Bell Tower

The Bell Tower was built in the center of the city in 1582. It is a two-story wooden structure on a square base with winding corridors on four sides. Ascending it, you can enjoy a panoramic view of the whole city. Not far away in the west is the Drum Tower which was built in 1380. Inside is a big drum for marking the passage of time every night in ancient times. Now, the Bell Tower and Drum Tower are symbols of the ancient architectures of Xi'an City.

钟楼

位于西安市中心,建于 1582 年,方形基座,木质结构,共两层,四面有回廊,登临其上可统览全城景物。其西面不远处为鼓楼,始建于 1380 年,楼内有大鼓,原供每晚击鼓报时之用。现在,钟、鼓楼是西安城的著名古建筑标志。

Greater Wild Goose Pagoda

The Greater Wild Goose Pagoda (Dayanta) stands in the Temple of Mercy and Benevolence (Ci'ensi) four kilometers to the south of Xi'an City. It was first built in the third year of the reign of Emperor Yonghui in the Tang Dynasty (652) for housing the Buddhist scriptures brought back from India by the eminent monk Xuanzang (602-664). The extant seven-story brick pagoda is over 1,300 years old. It is 64 meters high in a square pyramid wooden-like structure.

大雁塔

耸立于西安城南 4 公里的慈恩寺内,始建于唐永徽三年(652 年),是为安置当朝高僧玄奘(602—664 年)由印度取回的佛经而专门建造的。现存的七层砖塔已有 1300 多年历史,塔高 64 米,呈方锥形仿木结构。

Lesser Wild Goose Pagoda　　　　▷

The Lesser Wild Goose Pagoda (Xiaoyanta), built in the first year of the reign of Tang Dynasty Emperor Jinglong (707), is a brick pagoda of attic design inside and dense-eaves design outside. It rises 50 meters in 15 stories. Standing on the southern side of West Friendship Road in Xi'an City, it is, like the Greater Wild Goose Pagoda, a representative historical site in Xi'an.

小雁塔

建于唐景龙元年(707 年),是一座内部楼阁式、外部密檐式的砖塔,高 50 米,共有 15 级,位于西安市友谊西路路南,与大雁塔同为西安具代表性的古迹景观。

18

Forest of Steles in Xi'an
The Forest of Steles, lying inside the southern city wall, is the place where there are the largest number of steles of different dynasties. It has now become the Museum of the Stele Forest, housing more than 2,300 famous steles and inscribed memorial tablets of the Han, Wei, Sui, Tang, Yuan, Ming and Qing dynasties. The museum is the largest "stone-book warehouse" and a treasure house of calligraphic art.

西安碑林
位于西安城南城墙内侧,是收集历代优秀碑刻最多的场所,现已成为碑林博物馆。馆内藏有汉、魏、隋、唐、元、明、清各代著名碑石、墓志 2300 多种,是中国最大石质书库和书法艺术宝库。

19

20

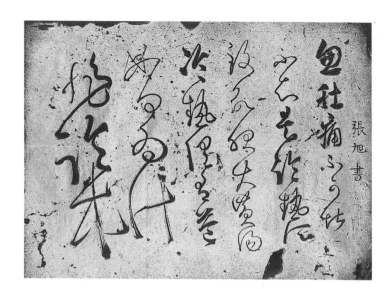

The Show Room in the Stele Forest houses tablets inscribed with the hand-writing of well-known calligraphers of various dynasties. The picture shows a tablet inscribed with the cursive-script handwriting by the famous calligrapher Zhang Xu in the Tang Dynasty.

碑林展室内陈列着历代名家不同书体的碑刻。图为唐代著名书法家张旭(生卒年不详)的草书碑刻。

The Six-Horse Carving in Zhaoling Tomb

It is now housed in the Stone-carving Room of the Museum of the Stele Forest. The Six-horse Carving was unearthed from the Zhaoling Tomb of Li Shimin (r. 627-650), Emperor Taizong of the Tang Dynasty. The tablet was carved in memory of the six fine horses which he rode on the battle-fields. The carving lines are bold and simple, showing the supreme artistic value at that time. The picture shows one of the six horses.

昭陵六骏

现藏于碑林博物馆内的石刻艺术室。六骏石刻出土于唐太宗李世民(627－650年在位)之墓昭陵,是唐太宗为纪念随他在疆场上出生入死的六匹爱马而命人刻制的。石刻线条浑厚简洁,体现了当时高超的雕刻技艺。图为六骏之一特勒骠。

The Shaanxi Provincial Museum of History
It is located on East Xiaozhan Road in the southern part of Xi'an City. This is a state-level modern museum with a solemn outlook of the Tang-style architecture, covering an area of 70,000 square meters. Displayed in the museum are tens of thousands of historical and cultural objects from the Lantian Ape (800,000 year ago) to recent excavations in Shaanxi. The museum is the concentration of the long history and culture of the province.

陕西省历史博物馆

位于西安城南小寨东路，是一座国家级现代化博物馆。此馆占地 7 万平方米，外观为典雅凝重的仿唐建筑。馆内陈列了陕西出土的自蓝田猿人（80 万年前）至近代的文物精品数万件，是古都西安悠久历史文化的集中体现。

（1）Three-colored pottery of a woman horse-rider (Tang) （2）Wine Cup（Western Zhou） （3）Gold-inlaid agate cup with the design of an animal head (Tang)

（1）三彩女骑俑（唐） （2）折觥（西周） （3）镶金兽首玛瑙杯（唐）

24

25

26

Great Flourishing Virtue Temple

The Great Flourishing Virtue Temple (Xing-shansi) lies 2.5 kilometers south of Xi'an City. Built in the Jin Dynasty (265-420), it was one of the famous places for the translation of Buddhist Scriptures in the Tang Dynasty and is also the place of origin of Chinese Buddhist Scripture.

◁ Great Mosque

Located in Huajue Lane beside the Drum Tower, and covering an area of 12,000 square meters, it is the best-known Islamic Mosque in Xi'an City. It was first built in the Tang Dynasty and was rebuilt in the Ming Dynasty. The distribution of pavilions, halls, towers and platforms in the mosque is compact and exquisite, blending the traditional architectural styles of Islam and Han. This picture shows one of the main architecture in the mosque—the Examining-Mind Tower. This wooden octagonal tower has three stories, and is the place where the Iman calls believers to pray.

大清真寺

是西安城中最著名的伊斯兰教礼拜寺,位于鼓楼旁的化觉巷内,始建于唐,明代重建,占地约1.2万平方米,寺内亭、殿、楼、台布局严谨精致,融伊斯兰和汉民族传统建筑风格于一体。图为寺内的主要建筑之一省心楼,三层八角,木质结构,是宣礼者呼唤教徒礼拜的地方。

大兴善寺

位于西安城南2.5公里,始建于晋(265-420年),是唐代翻译佛经的著名道场之一,也是中国佛教密宗的发源地。

Sleeping-Dragon Temple（Wolongsi）
The Sleeping-Dragon Temple（Wolongsi）lies on Baishulin
Street in Xi'an City. It was first built in the Han Dynasty and
still attracts many worshippers. Now, most of the Buddhist ac-
tivities of various kinds are held here, and it is the famous Ten-
Position Forest of Buddhism. Interior of the Law Hall in the
Sleeping-Dragon Temple (*right picture*).

卧龙寺
位于西安城内柏树林街,始建于汉,至今香火不断。如今西安的各
种佛教仪式多在此举行,是佛学界著名的十方丛林。右图是卧龙寺
法堂内景。

Pine Park

It lies outside of the South Gate of Xi'an City and is an exquisite scenic spot with pavilion and platforms.

松园

位于西安城南门外,是市内一处隽秀玲珑的亭台小景。

Xingqing Palace Park ▷

It lies outside of the East Changyue Gate, and is a famous place of pleasure in Xi'an City. This park was built on the site of the ruins of Xingqing Palace of the Tang Dynasty and covers an area of 49 hectares. In the park, Chenxiang Pavilion, Nanxun Waterside Pavilion, Hua'exianghui Tower and other spots were rebuilt on the model of the original architectures. It was said that "immortal poet"Li Bai (701-762) once drank wine and composed poems in Xingqing Palace, so a sculpture of "Drunken Li Taibai"is now erected beside the Caiyun Tower.

兴庆宫公园

位于西安城东长乐门外,是西安市著名的游憩场所。此公园修建于唐代兴庆宫遗址上,占地 49 公顷,园内仿原建筑重修沉香亭、南薰水榭、花萼相辉楼等景点。传说"诗仙"李白(701－762 年)曾在兴庆宫内醉酒吟诗,因此彩云阁旁有一尊"太白醉酒"雕像。

32

Flourishing-Buddhism Temple (Xing-jiaosi)

Shaolingyuan, 20 kilometers southeast of Xi'an City, is the birth place of the Huayan Sect of Chinese Buddhism. Built in the second year of Emperor Zongzhang (669) in the Tang Dynasty, the temple has a stupa in which the bones of the eminent Monk Xuanzang of Tang Dynasty were buried. Monk Xuanzang left Chang'an for India in the third year of Emperor Zhenguan (629) on a pilgrimage seeking Buddhist Scriptures. Seventeen years later, he returned with the Buddhist scriptures and devoted himself to their translation, making a great contribution to the spread of Buddhism in China. The picture on the right is a line-cut artwork "Xuanzang Carrying Buddhist Scriptures".

兴教寺

在西安东南 20 公里处的少陵原，是中国佛教华严宗的发祥地。始建于唐总章二年（669 年），寺内建有安葬唐代高僧玄奘遗骨的舍利塔。玄奘于唐贞观三年（629 年）由唐都长安西去印度取经，历时 17 年，取回后致力于翻译佛典，为佛教在中国的传播作出了巨大贡献。右图为线刻《玄奘负笈图》。

Mount Huashan

It rises to the south of Huayin City, 120 kilometers
east of Xi'an City, at an altitude of 2,160 meters and is
one of the famous "Five Mountains" in China. Mount
Huashan is famous for its precipitous and dangerous
peaks. There are five peaks and the south peak is the
highest. The path to the top of the mountain is very
narrow and steep. It has been a tourist spot since ancient times. The west peak of Mount Huashan is just
like a cliff and faces the plain of Shaanxi (*right
picture*).

华山

位于西安市东120公里的华阴市南,海拔2160米,是中国
著名的"五岳"之一。华山以陡峭险奇著称,自古便是游览
胜地。山上五峰并立,南峰最高。右图为华山西峰陡壁千
仞,雄峙秦川。

The Ruins of Banpo

At Banpo Village in the eastern suburbs of Xi'an, there is a fairly complete village ruin of the matriarchal society, important representative of the Yangshao Culture in the New Stone Age about 6,000 years ago. A great number of colored pottery products were unearthed from this site, and they fully reflect the level of production and the value of art at the time. The picture is a basin with the pattern of "human-face and fish-scales".

半坡遗址

位于西安东郊半坡村,是一处比较完整的母系氏族社会的村落遗址,为大约6000年前中国新石器时代仰韶文化的重要代表。遗址出土了大量的彩陶制品,充分反映了当时的生产和艺术水平。图为人面鱼纹盆。

◁ The site of ruins is divided into residential area, burial area and pottery-making area. The existing area is about 50,000 square meters.

遗址分居住区、墓葬区和制陶区几大部分,现存面积约5万平方米。

Skull Fossil of Lantian Man

Xi'an area was one of the birthplaces of ancient Chinese civilization. In 1963, the first fossil of Lantian Man was excavated in Lantian County, 50 kilometers southeast of Xi'an. Lantian Man lived in the Old Stone Age more than 800,000 years ago and was able to make and use rough stone tools to obtain a simple means of living. Above picture is the scene of the Ruins of Lantian Man.

蓝田猿人头骨化石

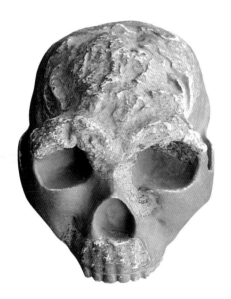

西安地区是中国古代文明的发源地之一,1963 年在西安东南 50 公里的蓝田县第一次发掘出了世界闻名的"蓝田猿人"化石。蓝田猿人生活于 80 多万年前的旧石器时代,会打制和使用粗笨的石器获取简单的生活资料。上图是"蓝田猿人遗址"外景。

Tomb of the Yellow Emperor
It is located in Huangling County, 150 kilometers northwest of Xi'an. The Yellow Emperor, also known as Xuanyuan, was a famous tribal chief in the area at the middle and lower reaches of the Yellow River in remote antiquity, and was regarded as the ancestor of the Chinese nation by later generations. It was said that he was buried at Mount Qiaoshan in this area. The picture shows the Xuanyuan Temple at the foot of Mount Qiaoshan.

黄帝陵
在西安西北 150 公里的黄陵县境内。黄帝号轩辕氏,是远古时代中国黄河中下游地区一位著名的部落首领,后被尊为中华民族的始祖。相传黄帝死后就葬于此地的桥山。图为桥山脚下的轩辕庙。

Hall of the Cultural Ancestor in Xuanyuan Temple.
轩辕庙人文初祖殿。

**Cypress Planted by
the Yellow Emperor**

It grows in the Xuanyuan Temple and, according to legend, it was planted by the Yellow Emperor. The tree is 19 meters high and measures 10 meters in its lower circumference. It is still flourishing.

黄帝手植柏

位于轩辕庙内,传说为黄帝亲手种植。树高 19 米,下围达 10 米,至今依然巍然挺拔,苍翠茂盛。

Temple of the Tomb of the Yellow Emperor

It was built on the top of Mount Qiaoshan. For many years, numerous Chinese worshippers from home and abroad have come to the temple to pay homage to their ancestor. A grand ceremony is held on the Festival of Clearness and Brightness.

黄陵庙

建于桥山之巅,多年来海内外华夏子孙不断来此祭奠先祖,清明时节还要举行隆重的祭奠仪式。

Maoling Tomb

It was the tomb of Liu Che (157-87 B. C.), Emperor Wudi of the Han Dynasty, located 45 kilometers west of Xi'an. Measuring 46. 5 meters high and of trapezoid shape, it was the largest among the tombs of the Han Dynasty emperors.

茂陵

位于西安西45公里,是汉武帝刘彻(前157－前87年)的墓葬,为汉代帝王陵墓中规模最大的一座。陵高46.5米,呈覆斗形。

The Tomb of Huo Qubing ▷

The Tomb of Huo Qubing is the most unique secondary tomb located one kilometer northeast of the Maoling Tomb. Huo Qubing (140-117 B. C.) was a brave and skillful general of Emperor Wudi and led his troops to fight the Xiongnu across Qilian Mountain. He died at the age of 24. Emperor Wudi gave orders to build his tomb in the shape of Qilian Mountain and to erect several stone animals and figurines in front of his tomb to commemorate his deeds. The stone carvings in front of his tomb were exquisitely done in a bold style. "Galloping over the Xiongnu"is one of them. In the picture the horse, 168 cm high and 190 cm long, stands over a Xiongnu chief who lies on his back with a bow and arrow in his hands.

霍去病墓

霍去病墓是茂陵数座陪葬墓中最具特色的一座,位于茂陵东北1公里处。霍去病(前140－前117年)为汉武帝时一员骁勇善战的大将,曾率军穿越祁连山远征匈奴,死时年仅24岁。汉武帝命人将他的墓修成祁连山的形状,并在墓前置数座石雕人兽,以纪表他的功绩。霍去病墓的石刻像刀法洗练准确,风格粗犷,"马踏匈奴"是其中的代表作。图中昂首挺立的骏马高168厘米,长190厘米,马下的匈奴主手持弓箭,仰面而卧。

43

Blank Tablet

This is the blank tomb tablet for Wu Zetian, standing side by side with the tablet "Recording the Deeds of the Emperor" eulogizing Emperor Gaozong in front of the tomb. But why the tablet is blank without a single word remains a mystery.

无字碑

是武则天的墓碑,与颂扬唐高宗文治武功的"述圣记碑"并列立于乾陵陵山封土前。为何碑上未镌刻任何铭文,古今众说纷纭,成为历史之谜。

44

Qianling Tomb

Qianling Tomb, located 85 kilometers northwest of Xi'an, was the tomb of Li Zhi (628-683) Emperor Gaozong of the Tang Dynasty, and his empress, who became the only woman emperor Wu Zetian (624-705) in Chinese history after the death of her husband. The picture shows the Sacred Way in front of Qianling Tomb.

乾陵

在西安西北 85 公里处,是唐高宗李治(628—683 年)和他的皇后一后来成为中国历史上唯一的女皇帝武则天(624—705 年)的合葬墓。图为乾陵前宽阔的神道。

There are many murals with unique features in the secondary tombs of the Tang Dynasty tombs. The picture shows the interior of the tomb of Princess Changle, a secondary tomb in Qianling Tomb.

唐朝诸陵的陪葬墓中绘有大量颇具特色的壁画。图为昭陵陪葬墓长乐公主墓的墓道内景。

Winged Horse at Qianling Tomb
On both sides of the Sacred Way at Qianling Tomb stand several dozen pairs of stone animals and figurines. Among them the winged horse was vividly carved in vigorous style. According to legend, the winged horse was for the souls of Emperor Gaozong and Wu Zetian to cruise in the night.

乾陵翼马
乾陵神道两侧排列着数十对石雕人兽,其中的翼马体态雄健,造型神奇。传说乾陵前放置此马是供唐高宗和武则天在天之灵夜巡之用。

48

◁

The Tomb of Imperial Concubine Yang

It lies on Maozai Slope in Xingping County west of Xi'an City. Imperial Concubine Yang (719-756), named Yuhuan, was the favorite concubine of Li Longji, Emperor Xuanzong of the Tang Dynasty, and was good at singing and dancing. When a coup d'etat was staged in the court, she was ordered to be executed at this place. Inside the tomb are many inscriptions by famous people of different dynasties.

杨贵妃墓

位于西安市西兴平县的马嵬坡。杨贵妃（719－756年）名玉环，为唐玄宗李隆基（712－756在位）的宠妃，能歌善舞。在朝内出现叛乱时被赐死于此地。墓地内有墓冢一座及历代名人的题咏。

Portrait of Imperial Concubine Yang
杨贵妃画像

Law Gate Temple

The Law Gate Temple (Famensi) lies in Fufeng County 120 kilometers west of Xi'an City. It is a famous temple housing the cremated fingers of the Buddhist patriarch Sakyamuni. First built in the Eastern Han Dynasty (25-220), it was destroyed and rebuilt several times in following dynasties. During a renovation in 1987, an underground hall was discovered beneath the ruins of the pagoda base in which more than 400 pieces of cultural relics, including four cremated Buddha's fingers, were excavated.

法门寺

位于西安市西 120 公里的扶风县,是奉存佛祖释迦牟尼真身舍利的著名寺院。始建于东汉(25—220 年),后朝毁建数次,1987 年整修时于倒塌的塔基内发现地宫,出土了包括 4 枚佛指舍利在内的珍贵文物 400 余件。

(1)Silver cage for swan goose　(2)Silver censer
(3)Seven-layer Treasure Box for keeping Buddhist relics

(1)鸿雁纹银笼子　(2)银熏炉　(3)放置舍利的七重宝函

②　①
③

Qingshan Temple

The temple lies to the northeast of Lingtong County, about 30 kilometers east of Xi'an City, and is a famous Buddhist temple from the Sui and Tang dynasties. A large number of cultural relics including porcelain, three-color pottery, and gold and silverware, were unearthed from the temple. Of them, the gold box for containing the Buddha's relics and its outer silver cover are 14 cm long and 21 cm long respectively and exquisitely carved.

庆山寺

位于西安城东 30 公里的临潼县东北,是隋唐时期的佛教名刹,出土了大量的瓷器、三彩器、金银器等文物。其中用于安置舍利的金棺和外罩的银椁分别长 14 厘米和 21 厘米,雕工细腻,造型精美。

Han Dynasty Terra-cotta Army

They are now displayed in the Xianyang Museum in Xianyang City 28 kilometers from Xi'an. In 1974, during the excavation of the tomb of Liu Bang, Emperor Gaozu, who was the first emperor of the Han Dynasty, at Yangjiawan, more than 3,000 pieces of colored terra-cotta army were discovered. These Han terra-cotta figurines measure 50-70 cm high including soldiers, cavalrymen and music band. Beautifully shaped and exquisitely painted, they are typical representatives of the Han Dynasty terra-cotta army.

汉兵马俑

现陈列于距西安 28 公里的咸阳市咸阳博物馆。1974 年,在陕西咸阳东北杨家湾发掘汉朝开国皇帝——汉高祖刘邦的陪葬墓时,出土了彩绘陶兵马俑 3000 余件。这些汉俑高约 50—70 厘米,分步兵俑、骑兵俑、乐俑等类型,造型多样,彩绘精良,是汉代兵马俑的典型代表。

56

Huaqing Pond at Mount Lishan

It lies to the south of Lingtong County 30 kilometers east of Xi'an City. Mount Lishan is a side range of Qinling Mountains 1,256 meters above sea level. At the foot of the mountain, there is a hot spring. Emperor Xuanzong of the Tang had the Huaqing Hall constructed at this place, and several bathing ponds were built inside and named the Huaqing Pond. There still exist the ruins of the pond and halls, towers, pavilions and other garden structures constructed in later dynasties.

骊山华清池

位于西安市东 30 公里的临潼县城南。骊山为秦岭余脉,海拔 1256 米,山麓有温泉涌出,唐玄宗在此建成华清宫,宫内设浴池数座,又称华清池。如今这里存有唐代浴池遗址及后朝增建的楼台殿宇等园林建筑。

The outside of the ruins of the pond in which Emperor Xuanzong and Imperial Concubine Yang once bathed.

唐玄宗与杨贵妃当年沐浴过的浴池遗址外景。

With the mountain at the back and river in the front,
Huaqing Pond is often enshrouded in mist and tranquil-
lity.

华清池依山傍水，景区内常常雾霭迷漫，景色清幽可人。

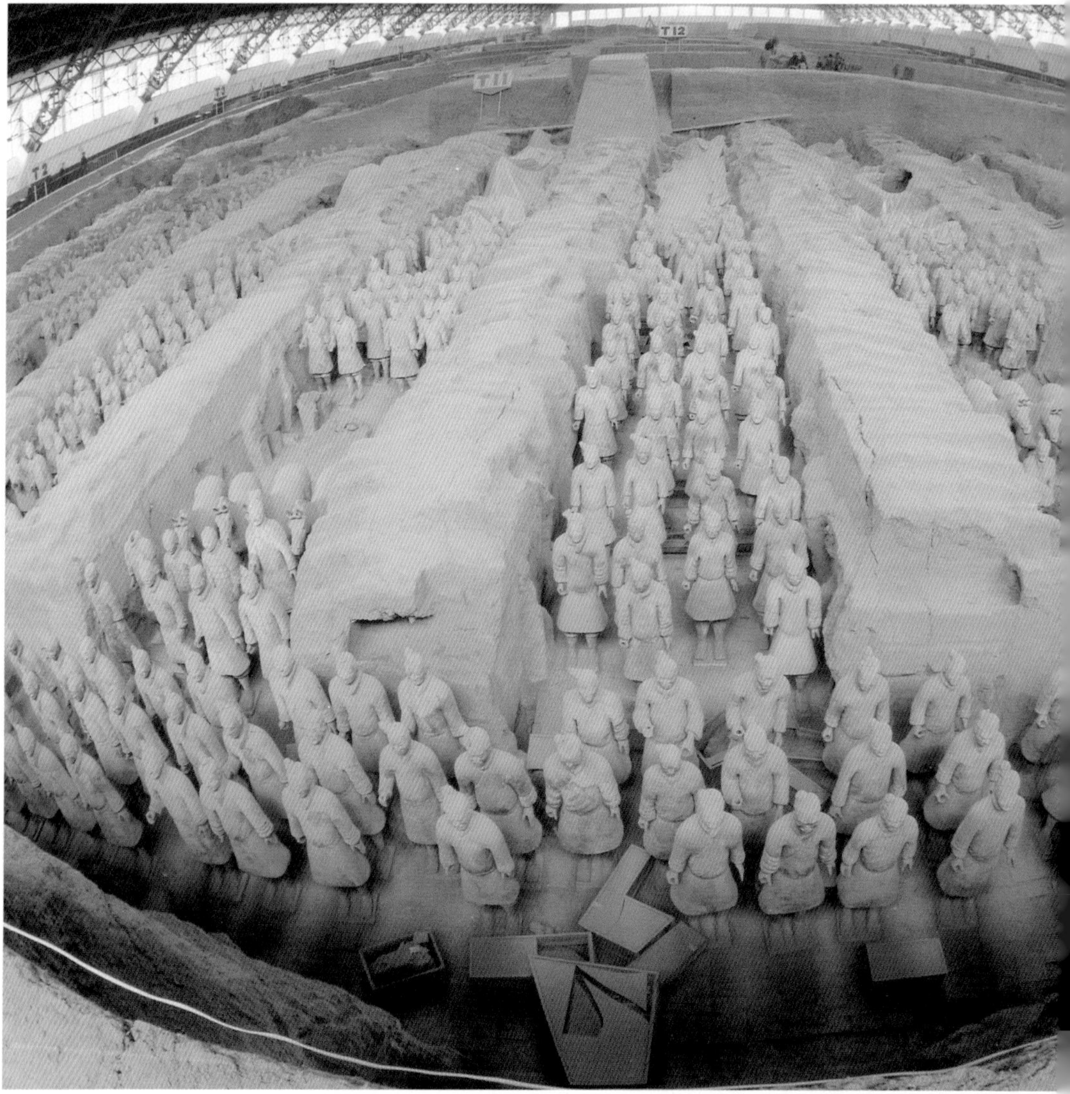
T12
T11
T2

Terra-cotta Army in the Tomb of Qinshihuang

A large burial pit of the Tomb of Qinshihuang (First Emperor of the Qin) (246-209 B. C.) was discovered in Lingtong County east of Xi'an City. The excavation revealed more than 1,000 pieces of pottery figurines, bronze chariots and horses and weapons. The discovery of this ancient civilization is known as the "Eighth Wonder in the World". So far, three burial pits have been found. The No. 1 pit buried a rectangular formation of chariots and army troops; the No. 2 pit buried a winding formation of chariots, army troops and cavalries; and the No. 3 pit was a command headquarters. Now, a Terra-cotta Army Museum has been set up for the protection of the discovery. The picture shows the scene of the No. 1 pit.

秦始皇陵兵马俑

1974年,西安市东临潼县境内发现了秦始皇(前246—前209年在位)陵的大型陪葬坑,经挖掘出土了模仿军队编制的陶俑、陶马千余件,以及青铜车马和兵器等物,这一古代文明奇观的发现,被称为"世界第八大奇迹"。迄今已探知的俑坑为三个,1号坑为战车与步兵排列的长方阵,2号坑为战车、步兵、骑兵混编的曲形阵,3号坑为指挥部。现已建立兵马俑博物馆加以保护。图为1号坑全景。

The carving of the pottery soldiers is very fine and true to life，but their features and hand gestures are all different.

兵俑的细部塑造十分真实，容貌和手势各不相同。

◁ A vivid army formation.
栩栩如生的兵阵。

The terra-cotta army troops are in the size true to life and in even proportion. There are soldiers, army officers, warriors, infantry, cavalry and horse-drivers. The picture shows a rank of cavalry.

兵马俑的形态大小皆与实物相仿,比例匀称,造型逼真。兵俑分将军俑、军吏俑、武士俑、步兵俑、骑兵俑、驭手俑等,图为骑兵俑。

Kneeling-shooting soldier, part of the infantry. They wear short armor, with one leg kneeling down on the ground and two arms pulling a bow.

跪射俑作为步兵俑的一种,表现的是军中的弓弩手形象。此类俑身着短甲,单膝着地,双手在身体右侧一上一下作持弓待命状。

The Bronze Tiger Symbol used for commanding the troops.

作战时用于宣令的铜虎符。

A bronze chariot and horse unearthed from the east of the tomb of Qinshihuang.

下图是秦始皇陵东侧封土内出土的铜车马。

66

Villagers in Shaanxi

Shaanxi people who live on the vast expanse of the Loess Plateau are simple and full of vigorous emotion. They created a unique country culture, and this can be seen from the decoration of their clothes.

陕西乡民

生活在粗犷开阔的黄土高原上,生性淳朴,情感浓烈的陕西人创造了别具特色的乡土文化,从色彩鲜艳,造型拙朴的乡民衣饰上可见一斑。

Fengxiang Bodiless Color-Painted Clay Figurine ▷

As a folk artwork of Shaanxi, it has had 600 years of history, with birds and animals as the models with exaggeration and rich colors. The picture shows a clay tiger head.

凤翔脱胎彩画泥偶

是陕西凤翔县出产的民间艺术品,工艺传统已延续600多年,以禽兽造型为主,形象夸张洗练,色彩浓厚饱满。图为泥塑虎头。

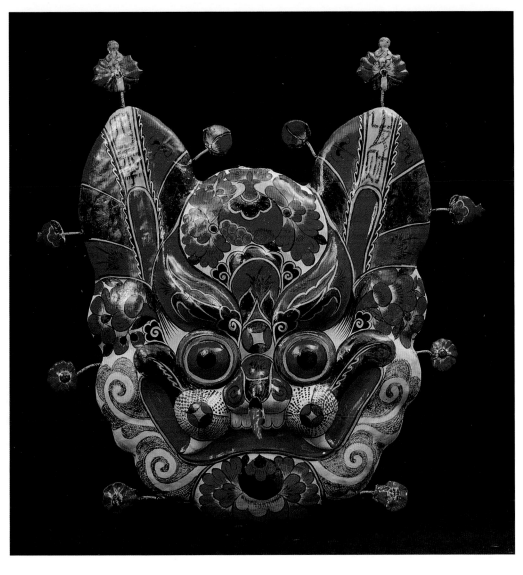

69

Making Flowery Buns

Flowery bun is a kind of food as well as a folk art, very popular in the countryside of Shaanxi. In the first month of the lunar year, on the Festival of Clearness and Brightness and on the Dragon Boat Festival, local women use scissors, hair-combs and spoons to cut and press flower, bird or animal patterns on the dough which are then steamed. They are used for worshipping sacrifices or gifts for relatives or friends, symbolizing luck, good wishes or warding off calamities.

制作花馍

花馍亦称面花,既是食品,又是民间工艺品,在陕西乡村地区流传甚广。在农历正月、清明节、端阳节等节日时,当地巧妇常用剪刀、木梳、羹匙等在馍(即馒头)坯上加工出花朵鸟兽等图案,上屉蒸熟后置家中上供或互赠亲朋,以表祈福、祝愿或消灾之意。

70

Cave Dwellings of Northern Shaanxi
The central and northern part of Shaanxi is located on the dry Loess Plateau, so that the housing in this area is mainly cave dwellings. The caves are warm in winter and cool in summer, suitable for dwelling. They have become the symbols of Shaanxi Province.

陕北窑洞
陕西中北部地处较为干旱少雨的黄土高原,因此当地建房因地制宜,在干硬的黄土上凿洞为居,称为窑洞。窑洞冬暖夏凉,居住舒适,成为陕西富有特色的代表建筑之一。图为内外装饰一新的窑洞和喜气洋洋的户主一家。

Traditional Festivities of Xi'an
They are a kind of folk entertainment popular in Guanzhong Area in
Shaanxi, performed by villagers in the first lunar month or on tem-
ple fairs, including drum music, firecrackers, stilts, land boat and
Yangge dance. The picture shows a stilt performance.

西安社火
社火是关中地区流行已久的一种民间娱乐活动,由乡民组织起来在正
月或庙会上演出,包括鼓乐、芯子、高跷、旱船、秧歌等多种形式,图中为
高跷演出。

图书在版编目（CIP）数据

西安：英、汉／曹蕾编撰；罗忠民等摄影．—北京：外文出版社，1998.11
ISBN 7-119-02245-8

Ⅰ．西…　Ⅱ．①曹…②罗…　Ⅲ．旅游指南-西安　Ⅳ．K928.941.1
中国版本图书馆 CIP 数据核字(98)第 26875 号

Text by：Cao Lei
Edited by：Ying Ren
Photos by：Luo Zhongmin　An Keren
　　　　　　　Liu Chungen　Lu Xin'an
　　　　　　　Qiu Ziyu　Lu Zhongmin
　　　　　　　Meng Zi　Yang Limin
Translated by：Linda Xu
Designed by：Tong Bo

First edition 1999
Second edition 2000

Xi'an

ISBN 7-119-02245-8

© Foreign Languages Press
Published by Foreign Languages Press
24 Baiwanzhuang Road，Beijing 100037，China
Home Page：http://www.flp.com.cn
E-mail Addresses：info @ flp.com.cn
　　　　　　　　sales @ flp.com.cn
Printed in the People's Republic of China

编撰：曹　蕾
责任编辑：应　人
摄影：罗忠民　安克仁
　　　　刘春根　路新安
　　　　邱子渝　鲁忠民
　　　　蒙　紫　杨力民
翻译：徐　林
设计：佟　博

西　安

曹　蕾　编

© 外文出版社
外文出版社出版
（中国北京百万庄大街 24 号）
邮政编码 100037
外文出版社网页：http://www.flp.com.cn
外文出版社电子邮件地址：info @ flp.com.cn
　　　　　　　　　　　 sales @ flp.com.cn
天时印刷(深圳)有限公司印刷
1999 年(24 开)第一版
2000 年第一版第二次印刷
（英汉）
ISBN 7-119-02245-8/J・1446(外)
004800 (精)